CHRISTIAN LEADERSHIP – DYNAMIC CHANGE

By

Rev Dr Isaac Lim

HEADLINE SPECIAL

Published for *Headway* by
MOORLEY'S Print & Publishing

ISBN 10: 0-86071-600-7
ISBN 13: 978-086071-600-6

British Library Cataloguing in Publication Data.
A catalogue record for this book is available
from the British Library.

HEADLINE *SPECIALS*

are published for Headway by

MOORLEY'S Print & Publishing

23 Park Rd., Ilkeston, Derbys DE7 5DA
✄ Tel/Fax: (0115) 932 0643 ✄

using Author's text supplied electronically

INTRODUCTION

We are living in a fast changing world. Global and technological advancements have changed the texture of lifestyle and communication. The internet has transformed access to knowledge and turned the world into a global village. Corporations and governments have made adjustments to cope with the new order of things so as to remain relevant and competitive. What about the church?

I worry about the church as I watch a world in transformation. I live in a city where changes are taking place all the time. Every other day, something new is being introduced to keep pace with global change. I read the newspapers and I see a government facing the challenges of a new world order head on. There is a sense of urgency to keep pace with global development and to stay on top of it. I see a government always planning several steps ahead so that the nation of Singapore will not be caught unprepared and unable to face the challenges that can turn the little island into a wasteland. I am inspired.

I was born in a British colony just after the war. I grew up in a small room of about 20' by 20' where my parents and six siblings lived. Poverty prevailed in many homes then. I remember clogged drains, floods, gang fights, slum fires, blackouts and beggars roaming the streets. Then a man by the name of Mr Lee Kuan Yew came along. He led the nation into merger with Malaysia, became the Prime Minister in 1965 when we were forced out of Malaysia, eradicated corruption, and transformed the nation into a world class metropolis.

John Maxwell is right when he says that everything rises or falls on leadership. Nations have risen and fallen because of leadership or a lack of it, and so have churches. I see this to be true in my country and certainly in all the nations I have chanced to visit.

God has an interest in leadership. When God wanted to change the course of history, he raised men and women to do his bidding. He raised Abraham to be the father of a great multitude from which was birthed the nation of Israel. He raised Moses to release the People of Israel from the bondage of the Egyptians into freedom. He raised King David, to establish and entrench the nation of Israel in the land of Canaan.

God grieves when leaders are not found to make a difference. His grief is expressed in Jeremiah 5:1 where He says, *"Roam to and fro through the streets of Jerusalem, and look now, and take note. And seek in her open squares, if you can find a man, if there is one who does justice, who seeks truth, then I will pardon her."* Again in Ezekiel 22:30, God says, *"And I searched for a man among them who should build up the wall and stand in the gap before Me for the land, that I should not destroy it, but I found none."*

Leadership has to do with the ability to influence people into a particular decision or action by persuasion. People are persuaded to act, change, transform, by the influence of a leader.

When we talk about leadership in the context of the Christian Church we are talking about leadership that results in dynamic change because change and renewal are at the very core of Christian theology.

The ministry of Jesus was a ministry of dynamic change. People were visibly transformed by His ministry. He saw change and transformation as imperative for any person seeking entry into the Kingdom of God and hence the Sermon on the Mount.

The theme of dynamic change was certainly evident with the outpouring of the Holy Spirit at Pentecost. The once fearful disciples were now transformed into giants of courage. They were visibly changed.

Paul understood the essence of dynamic change when he said, *"if anyone is in Christ, there is a new creation: everything old has passed away; see everything has become new"* (2 Corinthians 5:17). In conversion, God does a new work within us and we are not the same again. Change is a continuum from earth to glory and hence it is never ending.

Christian leadership has a dynamism to it because it is a leadership anchored in a God who works within us in ways beyond our comprehension. Paul acknowledges the power of

God at work within us. He refers to God as the One who by *"the power at work within us is able to accomplish abundantly far more than all we can ask or imagine"* (Ephesians 3:20). If such is the God we believe in, then there must be that constant expectation of change and renewal in our lives, ministry and leadership. This is certainly true in the life of John Wesley. From his conversion experience at Aldersgate Street on May 24, 1738 till his demise at a ripe old age of 87 in 1791, Wesley's life was a demonstration of innovation, change and renewal.

CHANGE FROM A BIBLICAL PERSPECTIVE

It seems to me that the underlying theme of Scripture is change. The Bible begins with change and ends with change. It speaks of a God whose expertise is creation, transformation and re-creation. It was out of chaos that God created the heavens and the earth. It will also be out of chaos and destruction that the new heaven and the new earth will replace the old (Revelation 21:1-4).

Because God is the God of change, His creatures are offered change and renewal as a life option. The people of Israel were offered the Promised Land in exchange for slavery and oppression. The raising of Judges in the early history of Israel was God's way of securing stability in the midst of anarchy. When the nation of Israel failed as God's light to the nations, God sent His only Son to be the Light of the world. Change meant the dispelling of darkness in favour of the joy that His marvellous light brings. It echoes the words of Isaiah who said, *"The people who walked in darkness have seen a great light; those who live in a land of deep darkness on them light has shined"* (Isaiah 9:2).

When the disciples of John the Baptist asked Jesus, *"Are you the one who is to come, or are we to wait for another?"* (Luke 7:9) Jesus said to them, *"Go, and tell John what you have seen and heard: the blind receive their sight, the lame walk, the lepers are cleansed, the deaf hear, the dead are raised, the poor have good news brought to them"* (Luke 7:22). He wanted John's disciples to witness a ministry of dynamic change.

1. Change is both internal and external
When change takes place, it is always visible to the beholder. Jesus' ministry was a ministry of dynamic change. It was not just a transformation from within. It was a transformation that issued forth in visible change – the blind could see, the lame could walk, the lepers cleansed, the deaf hearing, the dead raised and the good news brought to the poor.

Hence, the first thing we note about change from a Biblical perspective is that change is both internal and external. When Paul talks about conversion, he reminds us that something happens when Jesus is Lord over our lives, *"...everything old has passed away; see, everything has become new"* (2 Corinthians 5:17). What is interesting to note is that conversion results in a change of values. This change of values is manifested in the life of the person who is the new creation. His old habits and old values are replaced by the new that Christ brings. The inner change becomes externalized by a new lifestyle.

2. Change is not only personal but corporate
The change that conversion brings has a rippling effect. It transforms not only the "convert", but it also threatens the transformation of those around him. When the Samaritan woman experienced a change in her life through her encounter with Jesus, she left her water jar and went back to the city and said to her people, *"Come and see a man who told me everything I have ever done! He cannot be the Messiah, can he?"* (John 4:28-29) She was so excited about her new found Messiah that she was determined to convey to others in her city her new found discovery. We are told from the same text that *"Many Samaritans from the city believed in him because of the woman's testimony, 'He told me everything I have ever done.'"* (John 4:39) When change is dynamic, the community will experience the effect of the change.

We see the same in the conversion of the Philippian jailor (Acts 16:30-34). He and his household were baptized the day he made the decision to receive Christ.

Hence, the second thing about change from a Biblical perspective is that it is not only personal but it is corporate as well. When a person experiences conversion, it affects and infects everyone around him as well.

3. Change can be threatening
The third thing about change from a Biblical perspective is that change can sometimes be threatening. It can run against culture and tradition and violate accepted norms in order to usher in the new. Jesus was viewed as a radical because He initiated changes that challenged the status quo. The religious practitioners of His day were offended by His teachings and ended up crucifying Him. His handling of the Sabbath, His dealings with those who bought and sold within the Temple grounds, His practice of signs and wonders, His preaching and

teaching outside the Temple and synagogues, His feasting with sinners and tax collectors and His claim to be the Son of God ran against the grain of culture and tradition. The same is true today. Radical change can be threatening but it may sometimes be necessary to bring the church into relevance again and to wake her up from her slumber.

4. God raises agents of change

The fourth thing about change from a Biblical perspective is that God raises agents of change to do His bidding. Abraham, Joseph, Moses, Joshua, the Judges, David, the prophets, the Twelve, and Paul are some examples of change agents in Scripture. Jesus was a change agent. He introduced changes to Jewish religious tradition and mores and made His movement a distinct faith order. The change He introduced were so distinct that His followers were first called "Christians" in Antioch (Acts 11:26).

Change cannot take place without a change agent. Leadership is crucial in progressing change. Leaders in leading change become the voice of change. Hence leadership needs to be considered if change is to take place with the view of transformation and renewal.

CHRISTIAN LEADERSHIP IS TRANSFORMATIONAL

The essence of Biblical Leadership is positive change. The very character of God flows along the vein of positive and transforming change. He transformed a world in chaos and darkness into a garden of beauty and life (Genesis 1). As Halcomb puts it, *"God is a creator, an innovator, an entrepreneur who does new things, producing beneficial change, breaking new ground, pioneering new realities."[1]* God continues the same work of change and re-creation today in our world and in the lives of countless people.

Christian leaders are in the business of change as God is in the business of change. Biblical Leadership is transforming because the message of the Bible is life-changing. Change and renewal are the essence of transforming leadership. The Christian Leader is an agent of change by virtue of his own experience of conversion and renewal.

The responsibility of the Christian Leader is to move people from where they are to where God wants them to be. It is placing the community within the boundary of God's agenda. Leaders who are change agents see the transformation of lives within the purview of their calling.

Mother Teresa is a classic example of an agent of change. Transformed by Jesus, she leaves Albania and goes to India and works amongst the rejected, the destitute, and the dying. Her witness not only resulted in thousands becoming involved with the Sisters of Charity ministries worldwide, but also with the demonstration of what true light is all about. To millions of people, Mother Teresa pointed the way to the light. She became a symbol of a transformed life transforming her world.[2]

---

1 James Halcomb, David Hamilton, Howard Malmstadt, "Courageous Leaders", YWAM Publishing, 2000, p.20.
2 Halcomb, p.64.

THE HOLY SPIRIT AND CHANGE

Central to the work of transformation and change is the Holy Spirit. The Holy Spirit transforms both individuals and communities. It is interesting to note that during the reign of the Judges, God raised Judges like Othniel, Gideon, and Samson and empowered them with the Holy Spirit to bring about change.[3] It is said of Othniel that *"the spirit of the Lord came upon him, and he judged Israel"*; it is said of Gideon that *"the spirit of the Lord took possession of Gideon; and he sounded the trumpet..."*; it is said of Samson that *"the spirit of the Lord rushed on him..."*. King David received the Spirit's enabling from the time Samuel anointed him with oil. It is said that *"the spirit of the Lord came mightily upon David from that day forward."* (1 Samuel 16:13). In other words, the empowering of the Holy Spirit in the lives of these leaders enabled them to be agents of dynamic change.

The same is seen in the life of Jesus. We see the work of the Holy Spirit in the life of Jesus resulting in a ministry of dynamic change. Subsequent to His baptism and the descent of the Holy Spirit (Luke 3:21-22), Luke refers to Jesus as being full of the Holy Spirit (Luke 4:1, 14). This is further affirmed by Jesus himself when he reads the text in Isaiah to the people in the synagogue, which says, *"The Spirit of the Lord is upon me, because he has anointed me to bring good news to the poor. He has sent me to proclaim release to the captives and recovery of sight to the blind, to let the oppressed go free, to proclaim the year of the Lord's favour."* Then He concludes by saying *"Today this scripture has been fulfilled in your hearing"* (Luke 4:18-21).

Jesus, in reading the text in Isaiah was declaring His mission statement. The mission of Jesus can be summarized in one word and that word is "change". The mission of Jesus is to bring about change in the lives of people everywhere. It is not simply change, but dynamic change. This is what the Great Commission of Jesus is all about.

---

3 Othniel (Judges 3:9-10), Gideon (Judges 6:34), Samson (Judges 14:6) are some examples

Yet Jesus recognized that a supernatural commission required a supernatural enabling to make things happen and hence the promise of the Holy Spirit.

Jesus made it clear that the Christian's constant companion will be the Holy Spirit (John 14:16-17, 26; 16:7). In fact, in commissioning the Twelve to make disciples of all nations, Jesus promised a special enabling from the Holy Spirit that will make them witnesses to the ends of the earth (Acts 1:4-8). He told them to remain in Jerusalem until they were *"clothed with power from on high"* (Luke 24:49). The event of Pentecost made real the promise of Jesus and set the disciples ablaze for service into the world (Acts 2).

The change that the Holy Spirit brought in the lives of the disciples was evident in two areas. First it was evident in the area of ministry. The Holy Spirit enabled the disciples to minister as Jesus ministered. For example, Peter who denied Jesus three times was endowed with a supernatural boldness to preach the message of the gospel resulting in massive conversions. Not only that, with the same faith and boldness, he healed the crippled beggar by commanding him to stand up and walk (Acts 3:1-10). The supernatural enabling that the early disciples experienced was so evident that Paul talks about in his letters to the church in Corinth (1 Corinthians 12), Rome (Romans 12:3-8), and Ephesus (Ephesians 4:11-16).

Secondly, the area of change that the Holy Spirit brought in the lives of the disciples was in the area of character. The disciples were to bear the character of Jesus and the image of God. Hence they bore the fruit of the Spirit which is *"love, joy, peace, patience, kindness, generosity, faithfulness, gentleness, and self-control"* (Galatians 5:22-23). The Holy Spirit made it possible for them to be like Jesus.

The same Spirit is at work in the lives of all Christian leaders today. The degree to which His influence affects our leadership is dependent on the degree of our submission to His quiet promptings. His presence builds character as we face the challenges of work and ministry (Galatians 5:22-23) and His grace provides us the enabling to lead as Jesus led.

I like J. Oswald Sanders definition of a Spiritual Leader. He refers to the Spiritual Leader as one who "influences others not by the power of his own personality but by that personality initiated and interpenetrated and empowered by the Holy Spirit".[4] If Spiritual Leaders are Spirit-empowered, they are well positioned to bring about change as directed by God.

---

4 J Oswald Sanders, "Spiritual Leadership" Lakeland, 1967 p.20.

TRANSFORMATION OF THE HEART

Transformation of character involves the transformation of the heart. This has bearing in the way we do ministry. Whilst the gift of the Holy Spirit enables us to do the work of God, it is the condition of the heart that reflects the image of God. Christian Leaders in progressing change and renewal must reflect the image of God. Transformation of the heart is expressed in several ways.

1. Servant Leadership

Firstly, it is expressed in Servant Leadership. Jesus always saw leadership from a servant's perspective. Jesus did not look at leadership from the perspective of power or control but from the perspective of service.

When the disciples were squabbling over leadership positions, Jesus was quick to point out the difference between his understanding of leadership and the world's understanding of leadership. He said, *"You know that among the Gentiles those whom they recognize as their rulers, lord it over them, and their great ones are tyrants over them. But it is not so among you; but whoever wishes to become great among you must be your servant, and whoever wishes to be first must be slave of all. For the Son of Man came not to be served but to serve, and to give his life a ransom for many."* (Mark 10:42-45)

Jesus makes it clear that leadership is linked to service. The desire to bring about change necessitates a servant's posture which is a sacrificial spirit that will motivate others to follow with a willing heart. The towel and the basin episode (John 13:3-20), was an attempt to ingrain in the hearts of His disciples the principle of servant leadership. Paul emphasized the essence of servant leadership when addressing the Corinthian Church with these words, *"What then is Apollos? What is Paul? Servants through whom you came to believe, as the Lord assigned to each...For we are God's servants, working together; you are God's field, God's building."* (1 Corinthians 3:5,9)

Robert Greenleaf brought to prominence the practical concept of Servant Leadership when he wrote his book of the same title some thirty years ago.[5] He was perhaps the first to point out poignantly the difference between a servant leader and one who is a "leader first".

He wrote that a servant leader is "sharply different from one who is leader first, perhaps because of the need to assuage an unusual power to drive or to acquire material possessions. For such it will be a later choice to serve – after leadership is established".[6]

Greenleaf saw the servant leader as ministering with the view of making a difference. He says that the difference between a servant leader and the one who is leader first "manifests itself in the care taken by the servant-first to make sure that other people's highest priority needs are being served... Do those who serve grow as persons? Do they, while being served become healthier, wiser, freer, more autonomous, more likely themselves to become servants? And what is the effect on the least privileged in society; will they benefit, or at least not be further deprived?"[7]

The concept of servant leadership sets the foundations for broad-based leadership models relevant in the church as well as in society.

Larry Spears in "The Power of Servant Leadership" says, "As we prepare to enter the 21st century, we are witnessing a shift in many businesses and non-profit organizations – away from traditional autocratic and hierarchical modes of leadership and toward a model based on teamwork and community; one that seeks to involve others in decision making; one that is strongly based in ethical and caring behaviour; and one that is attempting to enhance the personal growth of workers while at the same time improving the caring and quality of our many institutions. This emerging approach to leadership and service is called servant-leadership".[8]

---

5 Robert K Greenleaf, "Servant Leadership", Paulist Press, 1977.
6 Ibid. p.13
7 Ibid.
8 Larry Spears (editor), "The Power of Servant Leadership" p.2, 1998.

Servant Leadership however is not a concept that exhorts weakness. It is a concept that claims the power of "other-centredness". As Anthony D'Souza puts it, Christian Leadership may be authoritative but never authoritarian.[9] He says, "When Christian Leaders realize they are under shepherds receiving authority from the Lord, the Chief Shepherd, they understand authoritative leadership".[10] Along the same vein, John Stott commented that the authority by which the Christian Leader leads is not power but love, not force but example, not coercion but reasoned persuasion.[11]

Servant Leadership is foundational because change and renewal must be wrought out of a servant spirit.

2. Mission and Evangelism

Transformation of the heart leads to a passion for the lost. As we grow in our love for Jesus, our love for the lost will also grow because it is for these that Jesus died and hence the Great Commission. Once when Jesus saw the crowds following Him, He *"had compassion for them; because they were harassed and helpless like sheep without a shepherd"* (Matthew 9:36). Jesus saw in the masses of people, individuals who needed hope and peace that the gospel brings. His heart reached out to each individual who came to Him. Such was His compassion.

We need to have the same compassion if we desire to bring the love of God to the masses. Mission and evangelism cannot be an activity of the church. It must issue forth as a Christian lifestyle birthed out of passion for the lost. We see this in churches that are spiritually on fire for the Lord. They see their mission as fulfilling the mission of Jesus as rehearsed in Luke 4:18-19.

Because of their passion for the lost, churches engaged in mission and evangelism are constantly finding new ways to be relevant. A church without a heart for mission will see no reason for such change.

Wesley understood the importance of mission as the lifeline of the movement he started. He declared the world as his parish. Not only did Wesley make the declaration, he lived it.

---

9   Anthony D'Souza, "Empowered Leadership", Haggai Institute, p.ix, 2001
10   Ibid.
11   Ibid.

15

The dynamism of Wesley is well known. The movement he began birthed a denomination reaching millions across the globe. His administrative ability enabled him to structure the movement into classes which sustained the renewal and raised leaders at every level. Such was the passion of Wesley.

3. Concern for the Poor and Need

The transformation of the heart enables us to see the world with new eyes. After all, this is the world that God loves. His love for us compels us to love the poor and needy regardless of race, language or religion. Transformation has a depth to it. The depth of change is seen not in terms of what we have received but in what we are willing to give. Change within must result in change without. Dynamic change takes place when transformation issues forth in our care and concern for others.

Jesus highlights this fact when He talks about the judgment of the nations that is found in Matthew 25:31-46. The ones rewarded in this judgement scene are those who through their lives have ministered to the poor and needy: the hungry, the thirsty, the stranger, the sick, the naked and the prisoner.

This theme of ministering to the needy is echoed by James. He talks about dynamic faith when he says, *"What good is it, my brothers and sisters, if you say you have faith but do not have works? Can your faith save you? If a brother or sister is naked and lacks daily food, and one of you says to them, 'Go in peace: keep warm and eat your fill,' and yet you do not supply their bodily needs, what is the good of that? So faith by itself, if it has no works, is dead"* (James 2:14-17).

Our greatest witness is to serve with no strings attached.

TRANSFORMATION OF THE MIND

Whilst the transformation of the heart is important, Paul reminds us of the need to have our minds transformed as well. Transformation of the mind is an important part of the renewing process. Paul exhorts us to be transformed by the renewing of our minds so that we may discern what is the will of God – *"what is good and acceptable and perfect"* (Romans 12:2). The thrust here is a changed mindset for the benefit of the church.

Yet, those of us who have been in the church long enough would agree that the church is generally not a place that welcomes change. The church would rather maintain the status quo than engage in change. As a result, the world moves on as the church nestles comfortably in its cocoon, distancing itself from the real world and becoming less and less relevant to society.

Tradition and Change
A transformation of the mind is demonstrated by an openness to contemporary trends and culture which do not run against the grain of biblical standards. There is often a tendency for church leaders to be narrow in their outlook. Leaders in traditional churches are often bound by history that they become fixated and entrenched in their ways. Outmoded methods are preserved at the expense of the new. Jesus understood this when He said to the disciples of John, that new wine is not to be put into old wineskins, otherwise *"the skins burst, and the wine is spilled, and the skins are destroyed; but new wine is put into fresh wineskins, and so both are preserved"* (Matthew 9:17).

Although tradition points to our roots and history, tradition can sometimes stand in the way of change. Churches are so glued to tradition that the introduction of anything new is viewed with suspicion. Old ways of doing things prevail and the new are rejected because they seem to run against the grain of tradition. It's like the Pharisees rebuking Jesus for healing the sick on the Sabbath or those who view contemporary music in the church as entertainment rather than worship. We need to see with new eyes so that those who see things differently can also be blessed.

In a world of change, the Christian Leader has no choice but to study trends and act on them. This is well exemplified in the world of business where trends are studied in order to secure first mover advantage. Should we not do the same as we embark on our Father's business?

Not too long ago, I was in a bookshop browsing through a section on Management. I was amazed at the number of books that dealt with strategic thinking, trends, and economic indicators. I saw a book on "Strategies for Asia-Pacific – meeting New Challenges";[12] there was another on "Regional Outlook – Southeast Asia 2006-2007",[13] covering political and economic outlook in the region,; then there was another on "The secrets of Economic Indicators"[14] which dealt with hidden clues to future economic trends and investment opportunities. These are only a few of the many titles to assist the business person plan strategically as he or she faces the tough challenges of the marketplace.

If we believe that we have something the world needs, perhaps it is time for us to consider where we are in relation to the Father's business and do what we can to win "market share". Was it not Jesus who said that the harvest is plenteous but the labourers are few? Should we not be about our Father's business in ushering change both in the church and in the world?

Wisdom is necessary in carrying out the Father's business but this must be accompanied by courage so that Christian witness can be expressed fully. We cannot just be satisfied with the status quo. Stagnation is an indicator of non-performance.

Remaining in our Comfort Zone
Transformation of the mind demands that we move out of our comfort zone into the realm of faith. Change is often resisted because of the church's tendency to cling on to what is tried and true even though they may be outmoded. Sometimes tradition is not a factor opposing change but successful methods used in the

---

12   Philippe Lasserre and Hellmut Schutte, "Strategies for Asia-Pacific – Meeting New Challenges" 3rd edition, 2006, Palgrave Macmillan.
13   "Regional Outlook – Southeast Asia 2006-2007, Institute of Southeast Asian Studies.
14   Bernard Baumohl, "The Secrets of Economic Indicators", Wharton School Publishing, 2005

past become a stumbling block to change. The argument is that what was workable in the past should be workable today – forgetting that time has moved on and trends have changed.

Faith involves risk. Some people rather the status quo than take the risk of change. Because change involves travelling on uncharted waters success is not always guaranteed. Peter Drucker identified three major risks in innovation:[15]

1. It will make obsolete current practices and patterns of operation.
2. It will fail.
3. It will succeed but in succeeding, it will produce unforeseen consequences that create new problems.

Hence, the risks in innovation explain why innovation is often resisted. We need to be entrepreneurial in our thinking.

Structure

Transformation of the mind includes the viewing of church structure with new eyes. The structure of the church which is meant to help the church achieve its goals can also be a stumbling block to the said achievement. Often, changes to structure involve a long process and this kills initiative and enthusiasm.

In mainline traditional churches, changes to church structure is dependant on the voice of the majority who are normally elderly church officers who see things quite differently from younger leaders who are normally the perpetrators of change. By the time change is agreed upon by the leadership, a few years would have gone by making the said change less relevant than it originally was.

Leadership Succession

Renewing of the mind has also bearing in the way we structure succession. Leadership succession amongst both the clergy and the laity will determine the future of the church and denomination. If leadership succession is not properly planned, the future of the church is placed in jeopardy.

---

15   as cited by Lyle Shchaller in "The Change Agent" Abingdon, 1972

Sometimes change is resisted out of self-interest on the part of church officers. Leadership in some churches remains the domain of the few. They hold on to positional leadership because that gives them their identity in the community. Younger people are not present to replace older leadership because the church has lost its relevance. Even when younger people are available, there is little desire to groom younger leaders with the view of leadership transference and renewal. Hence, the status quo prevails with an aging leadership at the helm.

LEARNING FROM THE JESUITS

Some months ago, I chanced upon a book written by Chris Lowney, a former Jesuit, entitled, "Heroic Leadership".[16] Lowney was a top executive with J P Morgan when he wrote this book. What Lowney attempts to show is the way in which the Jesuits organized themselves to face the challenges of each generation and how they managed in spite of great odds to bring about transformation and change in every assignment allotted to them.

Lowney ascribes the success of the Jesuits to four important pillars. They are:
1. The Pillar of self-awareness
2. The Pillar of innovation
3. The Pillar of love
4. The Pillar of Heroic Deeds

1. The Pillar of self-awareness
The pillar of self-awareness enabled the Jesuits to operate from a position of strength. Central to the process of self-awareness were the Spiritual Exercises. Each Jesuit recruit emerged from his thirty-day immersion in the programme with invaluable personal strengths, including:[17]

- the ability to reflect systematically on personal weaknesses, especially those manifested as habitual tendencies
- an integrated worldview, a vision, and a value system
- profound respect for other people and for all of creation
- appreciation of oneself as loved and important
- the ability to tune out everyday distractions in order to reflect, and the habit of doing so daily
- a method for considering choices and making decisions.

2. The Pillar of innovation
The pillar of innovation enabled them to use their creative prowess to handle new situations. They were willing to depart

---

16   Chris Lowney, "Heroic Leadership", 2003.
17   Chris Lowney, "Heroic Leadership" p.110

from classic religious traditions. As Lowney puts it, they were:[18]

- Embracing the world rather than retreating from it
- Praying on the run rather than in a controlled environment
- Striving for global growth rather than maintaining monastic traditions
- Basing ministry on opportunity rather than on strict definitions
- Finding God in the world rather than behind walls

The Jesuits were willing to adapt to their environment and culture in order to be relevant. They were quick to shake off the cultural trappings of sixteenth-century Europe in order to conform to the usage of the region where they lived.[19] They had the courage to delegate aggressively. They delegated responsibility to whoever could make the best informed, fastest decisions in the field.[20]

The Jesuits focused their energy on freeing recruits from personal obstacles to ingenuity. They saw three aspects of self-awareness as essential for pursuing personal ingenuity:[21]

- Indifference-inspired freedom from unhealthy attachments
- Knowledge of personal nonnegotiables: the values, goals, and ways of working that are not up for discussion
- Confidence to embrace new approaches and explore new ideas or perspectives born of a "whole world becomes our house attitude".

3. The Pillar of love
The pillar of Love was the cornerstone of the Jesuit order. Love was the lens through which the Jesuits saw the world. Love-driven leadership was for them:[22]

- the vision to see each person's talent, potential, and dignity
- the courage, passion, and commitment to unlock that potential
- the resulting loyalty and mutual support that energize and unite teams.

For the Jesuits, love was a transforming commodity. It was an

---

18   Ibid. p.137-149.
19   Ibid. p.150.
20   Ibid. p.162.
21   Ibid. p.166
22   Chris Lowney, "Heroic Leadership", p.170

expression of respect for human potential. They saw each person as uniquely endowed with talent and dignity and saw a need to allow this latent talent to surface and blossom. It was this pillar of love that gave the Jesuits great success in their endeavours.

4. The Pillar of Heroic Deeds

The Jesuits took three steps to turn their aspiration into reality:[23]

- First, they invited recruits to turn a corporate aspiration into a personal mission.
- Second, they created a company culture that stressed heroism, modelling the virtue themselves.
- Third, they gave each person an opportunity to enlarge himself by contributing meaningfully to an enterprise greater than his own interests.

Heroic leadership is motivating oneself to above-and-beyond performance by focusing on the richest potential of every moment. Jesuits characterized it more simply with their motto, *magis*: the restless drive to look for something more in every opportunity and the confidence that one will find it.[24] It is not the job that is heroic, it is the attitude one brings to it. The Jesuits were heroes because they brought a spirit of *magis* to their work. In the words of Lowney, "*magis* inspired them to make the first European forays into Tibet, to the headwaters of the Blue Nile, and to the upper reaches of the Mississippi River. For the Jesuit teachers in hundreds of colleges, *magis* focused them on providing what was consistently the world's highest-quality secondary education available – one student at a time, one day at a time. Regardless of what they were doing, they were rooted in the belief that above-and-beyond performance occurred when teams and individuals aimed high."[25]

These pillars made the Jesuits a formidable force for transformation and renewal. They brought change wherever they went. Such was the impact of the Jesuits. We can certainly draw inspiration from the Jesuits and learn from them.

---

23   Ibid. p.205.
24   Ibid. p. 209
25   Ibid. p.34

WHAT IS GOD SAYING TO US?

As we reflect on Christian Leadership and dynamic change, it is imperative that we seek the mind of God as to what we should be doing in our spheres of influence. Allow me to share a few thoughts.

1. We must seek God's vision for change

Firstly, change makes sense if a vision is God given. We must have a God-given vision that will compel our churches to action. They must see the urgency of change and the necessary steps to bring this new vision into reality.

John Kotter in his book "Leading Change" suggests an eight stage process of change.[26] His Eight Stage model is an excellent model in transiting change[27]. He believes that people are more likely to accept change if they can see the urgency and need for change. There must be a sense of urgency. More often than not, we are held back at stage one. We do not have a sense of urgency nor do we see a need to establish one.

In the corporate world, a sense of urgency is crucial in motivating the organization to change. Refusal to change can lead to loss of business, relevance and the sequential loss of jobs.

However, in the church it is not always easy to establish a sense of urgency. The leadership sees no need to create a sense of urgency and so everything remains the same with the general membership happy with the status quo.

How then do we establish a sense of urgency? Perhaps a re-examination of our mission in relation to the mission of Jesus may ignite a fresh sense of urgency to accomplish something for God.

---

26 John Kotter, "Leading Change" 1996, p.21.
27 The Eight Stage Process is as follows:
    1.   Establishing a sense of urgency
    2.   Creating the Guiding Coalition
    3.   Developing a Vision and a Strategy
    4.   Communicating the Change Vision
    5.   Empowering Broad-based Action
    6.   Generating Short-term Wins
    7.   Consolidating Gains and Producing More Change
    8.   Anchoring New Approaches in the Culture

Recently, I received a letter from Dr Randy Simmons, President of the Haggai Institute. In his letter he said, "In evangelism, Christians are just not getting the job done. The percentage of Christians as compared to the world's population has declined from 34.4% in 1900 to 33.1% in 2005."[28] If the world population is estimated to be about 6.4 billion today, we are talking about 4.28 billion who are yet to receive Jesus as Lord and Saviour.

If we believe the Great Commission to be the responsibility of every Christian, then we are far from fulfilling God's plan for the world. I have a suspicion that the reason why Christians do not feel a sense of urgency is because they are not fully convinced that Jesus can make a difference. If they truly believe that Jesus can make a difference, they would be telling everyone about the good news of the gospel. Our sense of urgency is linked to our belief in the relevance of our message to deliver a "dying" world from sin and death.

I watched an Independent Church in Singapore grow from 20 worshipers to 20,000 worshipers in a short span of 15 years. The average age of worshipers in this church is around 25 years of age. But their zeal for the Lord and their belief that Jesus can make a difference has resulted in many coming to the knowledge of Jesus Christ as Saviour and Lord. They have a sense of urgency.

2. Change must be soaked in prayer
If change is to take place, the process for the change must be soaked in prayer. Christian Leaders are men and women of prayer. When we look at the lives of great Christian leaders, we cannot but acknowledge the importance of prayer in their lives especially in transiting change.

Christian leaders need to emulate the example of Jesus who in the midst of a very busy ministry never forgot to be in communication with God. Very early in the Gospel of Mark we are told that *"in the morning, while it was still very dark, he (Jesus) got up and went out to a deserted place and there he prayed"* (Mark 1:35). Jesus made His personal time with God a priority. This is affirmed in Matthew 14:22-23, when after dismissing a crowd, *"he (Jesus) went up the mountain by himself to pray."*

---

28   He cited as his source the International Bulletin of Missionary Research, Vol.29, No.1

Why is prayer so important for a Christian Leader?

a. Prayer aligns us to the mind of God

Knowing the mind of God is imperative for a Christian leader and his team. This is nurtured through prayer. The life of Jesus exemplifies this. He knew the mind of the Father because He was in constant communion with Him.

Prayer is a relationship with God. This relationship is built up and strengthened through the avenue of prayer. John Wesley is a fine example of a praying leader. He knew the mind of God for his life because he was constantly on his knees.

b. Prayer gives us the boldness to do the will of God

A Christian leader directs his/her life in accordance to the will of God. The will of God may sometimes be unpleasant and even difficult. Prayer gives the Christian leader the boldness to do the will of God.

It was at Gethsemane that Jesus prayed, *"My Father, if it is possible, let this cup pass from me; yet not what I want but what you want"* (Matthew 26:39). And then again He prayed, *"My Father, if this cannot pass unless I drink it, your will be done"* (Matthew 26:42).

Through prayer, Jesus received the enabling to do the will of God.

c. Prayer allows us the wisdom of God

Wisdom is essential in leadership. Wisdom is the "ability to use your experience and knowledge to make sensible decisions and judgements".[29] This ability is enhanced when we surrender our lives to God and place our dependence on Him.

That is why the writer of the Book of Proverbs says, "The fear of the Lord is the beginning of knowledge; fools despise wisdom and instruction" (Prov.1:7). James in his letter says, "If any of you is lacking in wisdom, ask God, who gives to all generously and ungrudgingly, and it will be given you" (James 1:7).

---

29   Collins Cobound Student's Dictionary, 1992. p.649.

Prayer enables us to exercise godly wisdom as God bestows that on us.

d. Prayer exudes within us the love of God
Love is an important expression of Christian leadership. As we draw close to God in prayer, we begin to be more and more like Him. We begin to imbibe His character of love and our lives manifest the fruit of the Holy Spirit which is love.

Jesus reminds us to love our enemies (Matthew 5:43-48) and to forgive those who sin against us (Matthew 6:12-15). We may have enemies as we progress change, but we need to love them as Jesus loved them. Forgiveness expresses that love. Paul says the same, *"just as the Lord has forgiven you, so you also must forgive. Above all, clothe yourselves with love, which binds everything together in perfect harmony"* (Colossians 3:13-14). This is possible when we are closely linked to God through the avenue of prayer.

e. Prayer radiates the presence of God.
Christian leaders whether they articulate it or not are witnesses of God. They are either good witnesses or bad witnesses.

A Christian leader who spends time in the presence of God will carry the same presence wherever he or she goes. We see this reflected in the life of Moses. The Bible tells us of the shine that was on the face of Moses because he had been talking with God (Exodus 34:29). Christian leaders can radiate the same glow and be a blessing to others as they carry with them the presence of God.

A Christian leader cannot run away from a life of prayer if he or she is to be effective as a Spiritual leader.

3. Change must be properly communicated
If we are to transit change, we must learn how to communicate change. Poor communication by agents of change, have led to a resistance to change. People generally do not like surprises. They like to be informed about changes. They prefer being ushered into change than be forced into change. Hence the lack of proper communication becomes a stumbling block to change.

While it is true to say that some people oppose change it is not true to say that all would oppose change. According to Teal Trust (in info@teal.org.uk) reactions to change fall into five main groups

[1]   The **Early Risers** are those who enjoy change. They are the first people who would eagerly adopt a new craze.

[2]   The second are the **Early Adapters**. They follow the Early Risers once they are comfortable that change is a good one, or that it is likely to be alright.

[3]   The third group is the **Crowd**. These are those who would accept change once they see it become an accepted norm. With no strong feelings in favour or against change, these are swayed by the way the wind is blowing.

[4]   The fourth group is the **Legitimisers**. They are the slowest to be convinced naturally. These are independent thinkers who would carefully evaluate new ideas.

[5]   The final group is the **Resisters**. These are those who resist change from the moment they hear about it. They may be passive in their response, or lobby against change to prevent it from happening.

Looking at the five main groups it becomes apparent that the Legitimisers and the Resisters need greater persuasion than the rest. Whilst the Legitimisers may at some point come alongside the rest, it is the Resisters that may pose the greatest challenge. Hence proper strategies must be devised to cope with Resisters if change is to be accomplished for the good of all.

4. Our response as God's Change Agent
Perhaps the greatest stumbling block to change is the shortage of Spirit-driven change agents. It is time for us to respond to God's call for change. Change agents can make a difference.

a. The ability to Influence
The ability to influence is the very essence of leadership. The real test of leadership is whether there are followers. Leaders cannot lead if there are no followers. It is the ability to rally followers that ultimately determines a person's status as a

leader.[30] Title, position or judicial authority does not guarantee a person's status as a leader.

b. The privilege to Inspire and Motivate

To lead change, leaders can inspire and motivate. People want to be challenged and they want to hear a leader who can inspire them to accept a challenge. Highly successful organizations are often run by highly motivated people inspired by a highly motivated leader. There is a strong flow of energy in highly motivated organizations.

c. The discipline to Exemplify

Leaders who progress change can model the way. They can lead change with a passion and be seen as genuine and honest in their dealings. People expect leaders to be trustworthy, competent, confident, forward-looking, proactive, positive and enthusiastic. Christian leaders can exude an excitement that is consistent with their talk.

d. The confidence to Envision

Change agents are men and women of vision. They are persons of insight and foresight. They have the ability to interpret times and seasons and know what ought to be done. They are like the tribe of Issachar, "who had understanding of the times, to know what Israel ought to do" (1 Chronicles 12:32). As they cast vision, people are inspired to follow.

e. The grace to Encourage

Change agents have the privilege of raising a culture of affirmation. They refuse to perpetuate a blame culture that stifles creativity and innovation. Change agents know when to affirm and when to be assertive so that the change process can be realized.

f. The courage to Lead

Change agents are men and women of courage. They recognize their call to lead and so they lead. These are people of faith who believe that God is able *"to accomplish abundantly far more than all we can ask or imagine"* (Ephesians 3:20). Courage is a hallmark of a good leader.

---

30   D'Souza, p. x.

Courage backed by wisdom will give the change agent mileage in his ministry of transformation.

g. The boldness to take Risks

Change agents are risk takers. They are those who are willing to take risks if they know God has spoken. Joshua and Caleb were such persons. Of the twelve spies who were sent to the land of Canaan only Joshua and Caleb were willing to risk everything in order to possess the land of Promise.

CONCLUSION

The call of the Christian Leader is to lead change within his or her sphere of influence and beyond. This certainly is the thrust of the Great Commission so that change can take place in every life until we bow in worship at the feet of Him who is the Alpha and the Omega, the beginning and the end.

Christian Leadership is crucial in our world today. God looks for men and women who will be agents of His transforming love. My prayer is that you will be His agent of choice.

Let me close with a poem by George Liddell.[31] He wrote:

Give me a man (woman) of God – one man (one woman)[32],
Whose faith is master of his (her) mind,
And I will right all wrongs
And bless the name of all mankind

Give me a man (woman) of God – one man (woman),
Whose tongue is touched with heaven's fire,
And I will flame the darkest hearts
With high resolve and clean desire

Give me a man (woman) of God – one man (woman),
One mighty prophet of the Lord,
And I will give you peace on earth,
Bought with a prayer and not a sword.

Give me a man (woman) of God – one man (woman),
True to the vision that he sees,
And I will build your broken shrines
And bring the nations to their knees.

Will you be that man? Will you be that woman?

God bless you!

---

31   Quoted by J O Sanders in "Spiritual Leadership" p. 15, 1967
32   Italics in bracket are mine.

Evangelical Methodists in prayer and action

The aims of the movement are…

- The promotion of the renewal and revival of the work, worship, and witness of the Church, particularly within Methodism, through prayer and in the power of the Holy Spirit.

- The encouragement of prayer for revival at a personal level, and in the church at home and overseas.

- The furtherance of informed theological discussion in the Church.

- The furtherance of thinking and action on ethical and social issues in a responsible and compassionate way, based on the belief that the righteous will of God must be expressed in the life of society.

- The promotion of joint action with evangelical Christians in all denominations of the Church in local and national events.

- The promotion of mature Christian spirituality in the lives of all members of the Church.

Our basis of faith is that of the Evangelical Alliance, with a specific commitment to the Methodist understanding of salvation, as set out in the 'Four Alls':

- All people need to be saved
- All people can be saved
- All people can know themselves to be saved
- All people can be saved to the uttermost

Membership of HEADWAY is open to any member of the Methodist Church who is in sympathy with the aims and basis of the movement. Associate membership is open to those who are not members of the Methodist Church. Further information can be requested via the Publisher.